Saints
in Verse

Saints
in Verse

Frank Morriss

COLORADO CATHOLIC ACADEMY PRESS
Wheat Ridge, Colorado

PROSPECT PRESS
Sistersville, West Virginia

Published by Prospect Press
609 Main Street
Sistersville, West Virginia 26175

And

Colorado Catholic Academy Press.
Wheat Ridge, Colorado 80033

Library of Congress Catalog Number: 99-074626

ISBN: 1-892668-14-9

Manufactured in the United States of America

First Edition

10 9 8 7 6 5 4 3 2 1

Contents

Dedication

To my Mary who slipped away
Between dawn and waking,
Knowing perhaps that I should know
Where to find her when I may follow:

In Our Lady's court among the fairest folk,
Where tea and sweets harm not,
And words are warm and kind and laughter quick
And motherhood is known as golden gift.

There I may enjoy her soft voice again,
Speaking of things most, simply good,
And saying her rosaries as she did
When she was mine through many years,
yet too brief to know.

Saints
in Verse

Our Lady

All Saints' envoy to her royal Son,
    Heaven her cloak, its stars her jewels,
She takes their sanctity, her gift
    As proper tribute to His throne.

She walks with each the stony road
    From time's country to kingdom
Where time's unknown, and love's
    Light shows Love eternal.

Such light the saints reflect,
    Its mirror their souls
Receiving glint of it from her,
    Who so brightly magnifies her Lord.

Stephen (Protomartyr)

His dying words beneath the silencing stones
    "Forgive them," even as the Christ he preached
Had prayed from Cross before
    For those who persecuted Him,

Young Saul watching as cruel law applied
    Knew not the prayer meant him,
Nor could not have understood
    A Christ forgiving of His enemies.

Yet Saul himself is answer
    To Stephen's prayer of love
When meeting Christ on Damascus road
    He learned Jesus stoned when Stephen was.

Thus faith replaces covenant old,
    And Christ's Paul begins the way
That followed Stephen's steps
    In vast procession of martyrdom.

Peter (Chief of the Apostles)

No cock's crow was ever heard
    But Peter did weep again
As when he thrice swore
    The Prisoner was not his Lord.

Till finally on the hill of Rome
    Called Vaticanus, overlooking
All the world Peter paid the price
    That love thrice said exacted.

The devil had sought to sift him out
    And gather him into hell's storage bins of chaff,
But Christ had other plans for one
    Who would feed His lambs and sheep.

From Vaticanus cross hung unside down,
    Peter sees only sky above
Like blue waters of distant Galilee,
    And hears again his Lord call out to him,
        "Follow–follow Me."

Paul of Tarsus

Saul hoards stones from Stephen's pile
   To hurl cruel against the saints,
And rides all- hot to use them in Damascus,
   Knowing not who waits him on the road.

Christ, in blinding armor and at level unhorsing lance,
   Speaks to Saul now in the dust,
And demands cause of stones meant for Him,
   Which Saul had never really known.

Now Christ's Paul, purged clean of' hate,
   Conceives and leaves churches in every step,
And reveals Christ as gentiles' light,
   And long-awaited Savior of Yahweh's promise.

Michael (Archangel)

War declared in heaven by high angel,
    Burning like countless suns,
And sounding battle cry Non Serviam
    Against God's will for Uttered One.

Then Lucifer's peer, Michael, declares
    For divine Heavenly Prince, rallies
Angels left free of enemy's design
    And calls them to the cause of Trinity.

His sword-sweep of heavenly circumference,
    So none escape its shining command
That exiled angelic rebels forever
    From sight of proper home and joy.

And Prince from last parapet above,
    Watches as Satan and his hosts
Fall like burning, plunging star
    Into the light–extinguishing cauldron, hell.

Mary Magdalene

Seven demon-enemies of Christ
    Took possession of her heart,
Seeing her game fairer than the most
    To boastfully poach from royalty's claim.

She, a captive of their lusts,
    Using her beauty as their lures,
Is known as temptress, scarlet-clad,
    A test for even Purity itself.

Till look of love most clean and heavenly,
    Routs demons from their hiding place
And sets its flame within her heart
    Sure guard against desired return.

So Prince lays claim to pure white doe
    Intended for His gardens all along,
And there she is seen as favorite one,
    Among all proved by much love's test.

John (the Beloved)

But for Mother and step-Father,
    John alone heard Christ's heart,
The very pulse-sound of Divinity
    And rhythm of all Creation.

Reclined against his Master's breast,
    Taking feast of more than food
When Jesus turned bread to Flesh
    And wine to Blood to feed all souls.

Remained with Master when others fled,
    And stood beneath the Cross with Mary
To receive her as Mother and be for her,
    Son, exchange beyond imagining.

Thereby first of all disciples to come,
    Our stand-in at Calvary when Jesus
Shared His Sonship to God with us,
    Who, in John, take God to be our Father.

Zita

Saint of Lucca, servant girl,
    Served rich master, though
Served Christ more by work done,
    Duty, true, but means to aid the poor.

Gave too freely from her master's plenty,
    But earned signs of Christ's approval.
Gave master's own coat to beggar
    Which he had lent to her careful care.

Lost by that act, coat finds way back,
    Returned by messenger from heaven surely
So Zita escapes chastisement
    For charity beyond rebuke.

Patron of those who serve
    In kitchen, hall, or at the door,
Zita tells them a lesson well,
    To work is virtue, shirking a vice.

Not lesson less for everyone,
    That work spins golden dress for heaven,
Be it with hands and back bent sore,
    Or mind by genius or poet poor.

Peter Canisius

Noble recruit in Loyola's Jesus men,
   Throws words from mouth and pen
Into the fray to rescue truth
   From wild-wood beasts devouring it.

Snatched from their jaws it becomes
   Means to rescue the hungry ones
Deprived of Catholic nutriment
   By unending, wrangling civil war.

Peter's books and sermons build the wall
   Against an enemy's determined surge,
Using even stone or two recaptured and brought home,
   So much of Boniface's work still stood.

Clotilda

Wife to Clovis, king of Franks,
    Clotilda pursues his pagan soul,
Which would not yield to grasp of love
    Till one day Christ intervenes.

In battle Clovis sore-pressed
    By fierce Teutonic kin
Sees defeat at hand and in fear
    Invokes "Clotilda's God" to aid.

The victory his, Clovis, father
    To first Frankish kings, has
Saving waters to be poured on him
    At Christmas Mass in Rheims.

Clotilda, widowed, lives to weep
    At murderous contention of sons
And nephews for the Frankish throne,
    Sad seat of defeat and overthrow.

Yet Clodtilda, soon to die,
    Has final victory when God
Hears her prayers, and by storm
    Undoes sons' fratricidal war.

Edmund the Martyr

Boy king of Angle folk,
　　Fair knight of chivalry,
Pledged to Catholic piety
　　And to kingship as David was.

Must face invaders fierce,
　　From off the sea to Norfolk's fields,
Who hate his Church and would have
　　His people worship fierce false gods.

So Edmund stands against them,
　　But to fall into their hands,
Where, treated like Sebastian,
　　His body bristles with their arrows cruel.

Good king, who died defending right
　　And truth, until a kinsman,
Alfred came, and taught the Danes
　　Their gods of sword and shield were sham.

Pelagius (Pelayo)

Left Caliph's hostage as a lad,
    Pelayo keeps faith in prison;
No redemption by his uncle coming,
    He grows to handsome, holy youth.

Caliph hears, and woos him with wealth,
    With liberty, fine mounts and clothes, high posts,
If only he will embrace Koran
    And turn from Christian to Mohammedan.

"Christian I have been, I am, and I shall be,"
    Pelayo vows, and Caliph thwarted
Orders death for this daring child,
    Who fiercely tortured is set free by death.

In Spain remembered and invoked
    When other cruel conquerors
Would un-Catholic that proud land,
    Until Communism defeated as Islam was.

Therese (of Lisieux)

Little girl wishing everything
    Grows to nun embracing sanctity,
Whole and not by halves, yet
    Behind cloister wall seeks how.

Her ambition high as stars
    And wide as scape of universe,
Must be reached in menial tasks,
    Performed in Christ's obedience.

Sent His cross of suffering,
    She bears it silently,
Till, death-relieved, she goes
    To shower us with roses ungrown on earth.

Dorothy

Dear girl sees heaven beautiful
    As garden untouched by blight
And offering fruit and blossom
    To those who persevere in Christ.

And so she does cling to Him
    Like branch of His sweet vine,
Till sent to death, is mockingly beseeched
    To send a basket from that fair place.

She does to him who sent her there,
    A basket of fairest things,
But more she sends this pagan judge
    The gift of full flowering faith.

Ambrose

Bishop beloved, friend to everyone
    Except the Church's enemies
And despoilers holding high office
    Who felt the sword of truth he used.

Gave precious vessels' gold
    To ransom captives and gave self
To turn back invaders who would
    Ravage Empire and Church alike.

When Senators returned to worship
    Of their patroness Winged Victory,
Thinking to restore Rome's grandeur gone,
    Ambrose asks how a true goddess ever fell.

What need true gods of men's approval,
    Asks wise Ambrose; better to appeal
To One above who gives peace, prosperity
    To rulers and their people who trust in Him.

Nino

Christian girl taken to wild Caucasia
    Alone among her captors there
By miracles converts these Iberians,
    And then their king and all his land.

Thus faithful slave of Christ,
    Herself enslaved, set free a race
Bound to pagan gods and ways,
    Till churches rose, one her own memorial.

John (of Kanti)

Priest-professor taught students
  To defend their faith,
But gently so, lest being unkind
  They harden hearts in error.

He taught more by deeds,
  So open with what was his
That all he owned became
  The property of others.

His own body he saw
  As but a prison for his soul,
A prison that long held him
  Till he escaped one Christmas eve.

Good teacher at Cracow,
  Where candidates for doctorhood
Were long touched to that degree
  By doctoral gown of St. John.

Martin of Tours

Caesar's man, though pledged to Christ,
    Came riding to Amiens,
Caesar's cloak behind him, billowed
    With cold, cold winter's air.

Caesar's sword was at his side,
    Though locked in sheath for love
Of Christ, except as duty bade,
    By oath, taken, without heart's consent.

Now Martin looks down at Amiens' gate
    On begger gripped in winter's teeth,
Passed by by those well-wrapt in warmth
    Of body that did not warm their souls.

Martin dismounts to the cold city street,
    Unclasps Caesar's latch to free his cloak
And unlocks Caesar's sword to draw it out,
    And swing it sure in cause of love.

Cold sharp steel sunders cloak
    In two great parts—one for beggar,
One for self, each now half-warmed
    As Amiens folk looked on and laughed.

Oh, when Martin sees in dream
    That beggar, Christ, he knows
He should have given Him all,
    And so enlists by water poured.

Caesar's man no longer, Martin now is,
 Serving only Christ in quarrel
With Him against His enemies,
 By firm kindness used, not sword,
Until cloak was knit together again.

Agnes (of Rome)

Dear, pure baby ewe
  Gives self to Christ alone,
And for this virgin vow maker must die
  For her divine Bridegroom.

Pagans would rob her maidenhood
  But heaven guards this lamb
Allowing her to die for Christ
  Virgin still and only His.

Her chastity a thing of scorn
  To lechers of her age and this,
Not knowing that only the pure
  Can come to joy that never ends.

Beauty is given for beauty's end,
  To honor its Giver, Beauty's Self,
Kept imperishable where age cannot steal
  A gift that was not meant for loss.

Barbara

Girl of the tower her father built,
  In his absence has three windows there,
Signing it with faith in Trinity
  Though father had ordered only two.

Her windows invited light of truth,
  Into temple where father worshipped dark,
    hideous gods,
But earned for Christian daughter
  Death for daring disobedience.

Legend perhaps, this story of girl
  Who defied paternal wrongs
To be true daughter of heavenly Father
  But lesson clear of God's high parenthood.

Nicholas of Bari

Known to this day as gift-giver
  Bishop Nicholas gave something else
To heretic priest Arius–a slap,
  Before assembled fathers of Nicaea.

Fought without cease defending divine honor
  Of Christ, rescuing those condemned
By corrupt accusers, though innocent,
  And defending flock as shepherd should.

Nicholas continued giving after death,
  His body incorrupt, exuding sweet balm
That was a cure against disease,
  Proving him anointed by sanctity.

Polycarp

From Beloved Apostle's own mouth
  Learned the marvels of his Master,
Each word and deed remembered
  To disciples own with memory keen.

Thus the flow of Revelation
  From John to Polycarp to Irenaeus,
No truth added or subtracted,
  Seen as heritage for each generation.

So Polycarp would shut his ears
  To any teaching short or long of John's,
And so for disciple Irenaeus who learned
  Of Polycarp false teachers are Satan's sons.

Dragged to death at pagan's pyre,
  Beloved Bishop of Smyrna's faithful
Brings fire of pristine faith brighter
  Than that which made him martyr.

Teacher of truths no different than today's
  Polycarp showed Apostolicity no mere boast,
But rather unyielding felicity to that
  Which John saw flow from Christ's own side.

John Chrysostom

He turned his silver tongue as sword
    Against evil whether high or low,
Till Emperor's wife felt wounds
    And gains him exile from imperial see.

Great Chrysostom whose words
    Took precious metal's weight from truth
Like Christ is hated by those
    Who prefer fool's gold of lies.

Dying in exile John leaves world
    A vast estate of wealth proof
Against theft or rust's sure decay
    –the eloquence that serves but God.

His relics brought back then
    In triumph and honor by
Emperor son who undid as best he could
    The sacriligious sin of father.

Peter Nolasco

Noble heart pierced to its core
　　By those held prisoner-slaves,
Finds men to join him, ransomers
　　Of those in chains to Muslim masters.

Himself enchained to free another,
　　Leads Mercedarians bringing mercy
As Christ Himself had brought it
　　To all mankind which lost its freedom.

Now echoing from Peter's time
　　His lesson of self-sacrifice
May call to hearts to bring rescue
　　To those imprisoned in the womb.

Augustine (of Hippo)

Youth comes to Carthage,
    Keen mind burning to know
Secrets of good–but also evil,
    Thinking thus to be great master.

Yet is nearly mastered,
    Made slave to mind's hunger,
And fed false food as Adam was,
    Not knowing how it can poison.

Goes next in pride to teach
    In Italy's Milan, where
Thoughts and words and tongues
    Were given more honor than souls.

Until a boy's voice is sent him,
    Urging that he read St. Paul,
Where warning most dire is given,
    Against a life of wasted pleasure.

Then with faithful mother at his side
    Augustine turns all thoughts to God,
Takes lessons from the great Ambrose,
    Becoming doctor of Christ's truths.

Puts down confessions of his life,
    Admitting so much squandered,
And remembers greatest shame,
    A boyhood theft of pears in evil's cause.

Augustine thus gives hope to sinners,
  That repentance though done late
Brings more joy in heaven waiting
  Than saintly ones who never strayed.

John Francis Regis

Young Jesuit, denied his wish
   To go serve Huron, Mohawk, Iroquois,
Goes rather to the wildest
   Lost deep in France's wilderness.

Purchasing lost souls with coin of zeal,
   John is hated by the wicked and depraved;
With Christ protector, John prevails,
   Pouring out life's strength for enemies.

At last, the purse of energy spent at forty-three,
   John collapses, a last mission done,
And sees Our Lord and Mary opening heaven
   For him who spoke so well of them.

Catherine Laboure

Farm-girl of tormented France,
    Become daughter of St. Vincent,
Speaks with Our Lady in convent chapel
    On Paris' once-bloody Rue du Bac.

Told of sacrilege yet sure to come
    To city seized by Godless madness,
And of sinless Mary's mercy,
    Catherine becomes part of heaven's power.

Medal miraculous made known to her
    Shows Mary standing on the world,
Light flowing from her open hands
    To work conversion even of the Jew.

And Catherine herself, in death
    Spreads Christ's Mother's mercies,
When a twisted girl at tomb
    Is straightened instantly.

Jeanne la Pucelle

When voices call frail limbs to war,
　　A child of France obeys,
And though a girl, rescues prince
　　And nation from their shame.

But male weakness yet remains
　　To betray their heroine
As if embarrassed to be taught
　　That courage is affair of heart.

Such courage faltered in the girl,
　　But briefly so, till Joan, again
Confronts the enemy from execution stake
　　As saintly voices call her to Christ.

In Domremy Joan remembered was
　　For praying and sweet charity,
Even as she sewed and spun,
　　Perhaps a shroud, but surely a crown.

Hilary of Poitier

Pagan lore was not enough for Hilary,
    Who used up his youth in search
For truth, until some writings fell
    Into his hands–Matthew's Mark's, Luke's and John's.

And there He met God's words to men,
    That God who spoke His name to Moses,
And met His Son, He Who Is as well,
    One with and equal to His Father.

Now a cedar planted firmly in the truth,
    Hilary spreads branches of his mind
Beneath which others might find the wonder
    And the Glory of men's minds' light.

Truth's enemies begged the Emperor–
    "Uproot this tree from Poitiers," and
So Constantius did, seeking to silence
    All who held Christ His Father's equal.

Yet in exile did the branches grow, and flowed
    Words like flooding waters bringing down
The false fortresses of heresy behind
    Which hid those great but in error alone.

Then Constantius dead, Hilary returns
    To Poitiers, Bishop faithful, cheered
In his Cathedral by Christ's firm friends,
    Among them young Martin of the sundered cloak.

John Fisher

True Bishop stands against king's
   Usurping oath, paying life itself
The price for fidelity left unpurchased
   By his peers unfaithful to their pallia.

So Bishop and lay Chancellor, More,
   Offer blood encrimsoning their
Nation's flag, forecasting death
   Of kings to come, and laymen some.

First of a great procession of priests
   Who died to keep their flocks fed
The Body, Blood of Christ, which not Henry
   Nor any monarch could provide.

Fisher, who did not flee the wolf
   Set lose in land by royal lust,
But died to teach his sheep Pontiff
   In Rome is Christ in Galilee.

Thomas More

Sir Thomas knows God's will and king's
 Conflict, and all consciences put in hazard
To choose which master must be served,
 He chooses Him whose touch means royalty.

Last looking from the Tower's ramparts high,
 More sees the vast realms of Christendom,
And England dwindling down to only part
 Cannot survive in Christ if made the whole.

Henry, last Tudor monarch save for two,
 Puts Thomas's head on pike,
Not knowing his crown will soon fail,
 While Thomas wears his eternally.

Martin de Porres

Martin, conceived and born in shame at Lima,
   His father blushes bright at son's dark ebony,
Knowing not unwanted child
   Will outhonor him in Christ's chivalry.

Dark youth puts on white friar's garb,
   To serve all he can with humble skills
Of barber, doctor, nurse, concerned most
   With those, his color, slaves.

When admiring nobleman asks to be adopted,
   Martin demurs at being called white man's father,
To that man's shame, who answers
   He would boast of being mulatto's son.

So full circle comes in Christ's own time,
   To one disowned as a proper son,
Now Martin is sought, sanctity's master,
   To be father by soul's paternity.

Bertilla Boscarden

Poor little servant girl,
    Known as a goose, will not
Reject that name, but knows
    Even such can do God's will.

And that she seeks to learn,
    How a goose may become saint,
Her lesson first in convent scullery
    Scrubbing clean the pots and pans.

At Trevino hospital in world-wide war
    Bertilla ignores bombs and shells
To nurse the troops and show them
    The guarding Providence of God.

Armistice comes, but Bertilla sick
    Knows peace on earth but four short years,
Till the lesson learned of sainthood
    For a goose, she becomes God's dove.

Francis of Assisi

Sweet wanderer of Umbria's hills,
   Whose name means free, enslaves
Himself to Christ in all things,
   Bright, beautiful, whole or wounded.

And would give the world to them,
   But unowning it, could bestow
Only self, though touched to gold
   By Divine Alchemist's changing art.

So gathers those to him,
   Both boy and girl, who would
Possess but Christ as best of
   All beauty and world's delights.

Clare

She of the golden hair and high birth
    Learns from Francis noble is as noble does
And thus does all to serve true Lord,
    He who though King rejected was.

Determined to make her earthly bride
    Her family, friends would take by force
This fair beauty, determined freely
    To give all she was to Beauty's Self.

This great lesson finally learned
    From Clare, mother and sister come
To join her in cloister where Divine Lover
    Waits for all who seek the highest heart.

Benedict (the Black)

Freed slave, friar cook when not at prayer,
    Could not hide sanctity,
And came to be revered by all
    Who once was mocked as lowsome Black.

Ignorant of letters, illiterate,
    Benedict did read men's hearts,
Became superior under obedience,
    Taught sacred things by heavenly light.

Glad to be released, a cook again,
    The Holy Black counsels well,
Virtue is not in eating nothing,
    But eating little when desiring more.

Antony of Padua

Friar Antony, silent in all humility,
  Until obedience orders him to preach,
And light pours out like silver stream,
  Drawing even father Francis' praise.

All charmed by holy eloquence
  Flock when Antony comes to speak,
Shops closed, pockets and purses left safe,
  Sinners and scoffers kneel at his feet.

Wonder-worker then and ever since,
  Doctor of the Church, patron of the poor,
Antony is said to have found
  The Infant Jesus nestled to his heart.

Louis (King)

Kingly king and father to his people
    Louis serves with holiness
And faith so firm he worries that
    Such has merit without challenge.

He teaches poverty of spirit
    And sweet charity to his nobles,
And practicing that takes cross
    In crusade from which he goes to higher King above.

France which dared to kill its king,
    Successor to Louis, did it recall
That saint who would have died for it
    When enemy robbed it of sovereignty?

Mary di Rosa

Long before this age of laity,
    Mary worked long to serve
All in need, poor of spirit
    And of body–workers sick, wounded.

Did what religious could not do,
    And in doing disproves the lie
That Church before had no use
    For purposes of her laity.

Later as nun leads sister-nurses
    To the battlefield, where wounded
Were given succouring care
    By true Handmaids of Charity.

Vowed never to let chance go by
    To give aid or comfort as she could,
Her calling from time of girlhood
    To comfort all afflicted by this world.

Catherine (of Siena)

Strange Siena lass, rapt in view
    Of Church's need, calls all to follow
In the cause of Christ and Vicar,
    Though she small ewe amongst their flock.

Learned prayer early, making stair-steps
    Her kneelers when only six,
Catherine on the road, sees Christ
    With Peter and John–becoming His.

Thus when Church is ill served
    By high servants of that Christ of hers,
Catherine speaks out in flaming words
    Rebuking those who should be firm.

Calls Peter's successors back to Rome,
    Away from Avignon's tempting refuge,
Catherine teaches lesson not to forget
    That office in His kingdom offers Cross.

Justin Martyr

Turning mind to truth's quest,
    Justin encounters Christ
As Truth itself, so ending search
    Becomes Christ's champion at every challenge.

This clatter, clash, clang of his
    Commitment ends in court at Rome,
Where Justin argues still, that
    Serving truth and Christ are one.

Will you so serve, the judge demands
    Though torture, death be its reward?
Justin claims the greater prize beyond,
    And puts life as price for what mind has found.

Believers still, when told their faith
    A thing of mere desire and dream
Cite Justin to prove that truth,
    Philosophy meet in Faith's Reality.

Aloysius (Gonzaga)

Young nobleman, marquis by right as heir,
　　Instead renounces all to serve but Christ.
Spurns all pleas of father and nobles,
　　To learn humility as kitchen help, a Jesuit.

The plague comes to Rome and Aloysius
　　Begs to join the others, serving
The stricken even as they died,
　　Bathing, comforting them till the very end.

Frail Aloysius stricken, though not to death,
　　Foresees the end not far away,
Which comes that spring at twenty-three,
　　And comes bearing coronet to wear
　　　　in his Lord's court.

Luke

Dear physician, beloved of his patient,
　　Paul, writes of Christ's birth
In Bethlehem and gives the world
　　The homely wonders of Nativity.

Portrays Mary, her greatness and her sorrows,
　　Her son who blesses children,
Magnifies a widow's generosity,
　　And Risen, comforts first the
　　　　women of His company.

As doctor, writer, artist, Luke
　　Applies compassion to all in need,
Prescribes Christ the Healer,
　　At whose word all ills are cured.

Hyacinth

Apostle to his fellow Poles,
    And east and northward as well,
Hyacinth sees his monasteries
    Ravaged by the Golden Horde.

But rebuilds again where monks
    May pray and learn the one sure way
To lay claim to heaven, the seal
    Of its ownership the deed of holy poverty.

Dismas (Good Thief)

Christ's redeeming precious blood
   Baptizes first this criminal,
Who by God's grace sees his Savior
   Hanging there so undeservedly.

Faith comes bringing justice
   That outdoes any of men's courts
And changed the sentence of death
   To reward of life eternal.

What Christ had promised for all who would believe
   He first gives this man condemned,
Setting him free by pardon divine,
   To be Christ's brother in heaven forever.

On Calvary overlooking all the world
   Death was deposed as master,
And dying on the hill called Skull
   Christ wages war with it–and wins.

What better patron can the dying have,
   Who under death decree for sin,
Can ask for mercy even as Dismas did,
   Knowing Christ came to save,
      and not condemn?

Elizabeth of Hungary

Dear child bride, so loving
    by noble nature, more by art
Of Christ, who said see Him
    In others, their need yours.

So does she care, with husband's blessing,
    For sick and ailing, making
Hospices her castle, their suffering hers,
    Till widowed in young motherhood.

With Louis gone forever on crusade,
    Sweet Elizabeth weds herself to God,
Exiles herself forever in husband's land,
    Awaiting death to take her there to him.

It comes measured in the hours of Christ,
    His Passion her comfort, His promise
Her release, till, the stone rolled back,
    She goes, not twenty-four, in search
        of bridegrooms, both.

Patrick

The pebbled voices of his captivity
  Followed Patrick in his escape,
Calling him back to where he had
  Gone unwillingly, the loot of pirates.

Until no longer boy nor youth, but Bishop
  Patrick returns to Erin at
The Paschal time, when fire is lit,
  But in Druid feast kept dark.

The flame of Christ leaps high on
  Irish hill, till seen by all,
The pagan darkness is dispersed
  And Irish folk are Christ's.

The captive Patrick now captor
  Of an island's faith, sends out
His captive sons and daughters wide,
  Bearing the flame he brought to them
    one Easter time.

Oliver Plunket

Sent by Pope to Patrick's see,
    Armagh's Archbishop is wound about
By serpents of betrayal, bigotry
    That delivered him to mock court of enemies.

Called traitor to Stuart king,
    Oliver like More before
Dies proclaiming loyalty and innocence,
    Unmeaning plea to hating judge.

The faith that brought sweet Christ
    To Ireland and Albion alike
Outlived the hate set loose by lust,
    And Oliver is saint in both those isles.

Laurence O'Toole
(Lorcan Ua Tuathail)

Gave himself from boyhood for the Irish people,
    Comes to stand as Dublin's shepherd
Against Irish traitor Dermot McMurrogh
    Who had held him hostage as a boy.

Between high king Rory O'Conor
    And the Plantagenet who rid
Himself of Becket by murder
    Laurence is the Pope's mediator.

Serving that cause Laurence
    Seeks out Henry in Normandy,
To ask safe passage home to Erin,
    But stricken, finds grave abroad.

Poor Ireland, left a pawn
    Of bigotry and high ambitions,
Loses her own kings and chieftains
    But not the faith which outlived
        the strangers' will.

Margaret (of Cōrtona)

Wayward girl, runaway from home
   Seeking love in suitor's castle,
Breaks God's laws to bear a son
   Sired in desire, not vows.

Murderous sin overtakes father,
   So Margaret left without protector,
Finally repentent finds shelter
   For her heart in heavenly love.

Now she the suitor, Margaret seeks
   Embrace of only Christ, who calls
Her on His mission to sinners
   That none may lack chance to repent.

As Magdalen daughter of St. Francis,
   Margaret turns the feet of those
Running away from Him, true Love,
   Until they weep like she at Savior's feet.

Onesimus

Runaway slave escapes his master,
    Only to be caught by Christ's
Slave, Paul of Tarsus, in Rome,
    Where all things come together.

Paul the prisoner begets Onesimus
    As his son in Christ, and pleads
Freedom and forgiveness of former
    Master, sending slave home as brother.

Thus in baptism of charity is slave
    Now set free by that which alone
Cannot be ordered or owned, hearts
    Freely given, now divinely held.

Owner and slave the same, such
    Captivity a thing of boast
That makes servitude in cause of
    Christ sweet yoke and burden light.

Cuthman

Saxon lad, loved mother next to God,
    And cared for her through
Saxon shires and fields, a cart
    Her seat and he its harnessed steed.

Till both found in fair Sussex meadow,
    A place to settle, where Cuthman
Built for mother a cottage for her rest,
    Next to it a church for prayer.

Could son do more with wealth
    Than Cuthman did with love,
A charity continuing in cures
    Done to those admiring Cuthman's work?

Cart, cottage, church, all signs
    Of son's love for mother,
Each built for her, but more–
    A path from Sussex up to heaven.

Cyril (of Alexandria)

Cyril cast challenge against error
    Rising up in Antioch that would
Find two Christs where there is only One.
    And take from Mary God's maternity.

Thus Alexandrine bishop the Pope's choice
    To stand against Nestorius
With full force of Church assembled
    At Mary's final home, old Ephesus.

The faithful's chant outside
    Joins with Cyril's argument within,
The Word Incarnate was what Mary bore,
    And so Council swears her divine Motherhood.

God calls in every age till now
    Brave champions against proud error's boast
And though such heroes oft get wounds
    As Cyril did, theirs too the victory.

Rose of Lima

Little Rose, lived in a garden,
    Its finest flower, blooming there
With crimson-petaled beauty earned
    Battling self-will and hellish whispers.

Crowned her head with silver thorns
    Seeking to share with Christ
What sin imposed, though undeserved,
    And thus become His suffering one.

Rejoiced in dying anguish seen
    As fare to God's kingdom there
Amidst the pure white stars
    Glowing bright flowers of heaven's fields.

Donald (of Ogilvie)

All of Clan Donald have patron
    Venerable as husband, father
Of nine daughters, who on mother's death
    Live together under his tutelage.

Remembering them, hills, hummocks
    High spots in Scotland
Now known as "Nine Maidens,"
    Multiplied like loaves once were.

Francis Solano

Holy Franciscan, gives self to others,
　First plague stricken in Granada,
Then to Black slaves on storm-doomed
　Ship of passage bound for Peru.

Brought Christ to New World's
　Jungle-hidden tribes planting
Missions for them where before
　Only wildest growth had been.

Ends years administering what
　He had brought about, Francis
Would play his lute at Mary's statue
　Till called to where she dwells with Son.

John Gaulbert

Noble son burning to avenge
His brother's murder
Corners culprit and moves
To kill him now—but stops.

The man has made a cross,
And John thinks of Christ
Who forgave all enemies
And charged His followers do the same.

Thus extending mercy, John led
By heaven to monastery
Gives own life thus saved
By mercy to saving others.

With healing touch John
Succors poor and sick alike,
Refusing priesthood's honor,
Once fierce man, now meekest one.

Bernard

Scholar, contemplative, learns
    Lessons more of heart and soul
Than mind, one coming in vision
    Of dear Baby Christ in Bethlehem.

From that moment on Bernard
    Gives special love to Him,
Though high God, became mere man
    And suffered thus as one of us.

And Bernard suffered too,
    Seeing an ungrateful world
Torn by strife, unfaithfulness,
    And prayed for death as merciful release.

Thus may a saint find martyrdom
    In seeing goodness scorned and overcome
By those who choose like animals
    Favoring filth to shun the heavenly feast.

Andrew (Tribune)

Andrew and his men in arms
  Invoke Christ and are given
Victory against the Persians
  When serving cruel Emperor Diocletian.

Respond with faith and gratitude,
  Seeking baptism, enlisting then
As soldiers of Christ with oath of love,
  Which makes of even heroes criminals.

And thus comes the martyrs' reward
  Which is the badge of victory
Greater than that battle awards,
  To stand as guards at throne of Lord.